PoEmotions
GOD
& FAITH

PATRICK L.C. MEADE

Copyright © 2020 Patrick L.C. Meade.

All rights reserved. No part of this book may be reproduced, stored, or transmitted by any means—whether auditory, graphic, mechanical, or electronic—without written permission of both publisher and author, except in the case of brief excerpts used in critical articles and reviews. Unauthorized reproduction of any part of this work is illegal and is punishable by law.

ISBN: 978-1-950685-48-6

In loving memory of Elder Irvin Lyrell George, Reverend Mary Veronica Harris, and Reverend Irma Aitcheson—three pillars of faith who were proud soldiers for Christ during their lives. May they rest in paradise.

Thank you for your support
Enjoy!
Be blessed

Contents

Dedications ix
Preface xi
Introit...xiii

Love Like Nature 1

Let it Flow..3
Evergreen 5
Let it Roam..7
Let it Soar 9
Let it Burn..11
The Purest Love 13

Come to Him...15

He Is Able 17
Enough...18
Be..19
The Strongest Love...20
No Divorce...21
Everlasting...22
This World 23
What We Should Do 24
How To Love 25
For Us 26
God Force 27

POEMS OF FAITH AND REASSURANCE 29

What You Need to Hear 31
God Still Loves You 33
Deliverance 34
Better 35
Young People 36
In the Place of your Pain 38
Encourage Me 41
Be Grateful 43
Trouble Don't Last 44
Walk On 46
For Every Faith 47
For Every Race 48
There Will Be Days 49

POEMS OF JESUS 51

Who Am I? (I am God!) 52
Superstar 54
The Powers of Jesus 56

DEDICATED TO THE VICTIMS OF COVID-19 59

From a Distance 63
When This Passes 64
Appreciated 65

My Testimonials 67

Church on the Corner 69
Give Me Strength 71
High on God 72
Dear Godfather 74

My Prayers 75

911 Emergency II 77
Come to Me 79
For My Family 81
For My Friends 82
For the Dead 85
For Kendall 86
For America 89
For the World 91
For My Unborn Children 92

Living Until the End 93

I've Got More Living to Do 95
Surviving the World 97

About the Author 99

Dedications

This book is also dedicated to those that were affected by the COVID-19 Pandemic of 2020. From those that survived this disease to the families that lost a loved one, I hope and pray that the words in this book provide you with some kind of comfort during dark days. For those that work on the front lines (doctors, nurses, home health aides, EMTs, supermarket managers, teachers, daycare workers, etc.), if you did not feel appreciated before the pandemic broke out, know that you are so much more appreciated now.

Keep your faith and know that God loves you.

Preface

This set of *PoEmotions* is divided into parts, following the *Introit*, which hold particular significance when it comes to how many are in each. *Love Like Nature* contains six poems, symbolizing the six days in which God created the earth. All of the poems reference love in some way because God created the world we live in out of His great love. *Come to Him* has eleven poems to represent The Ten Commandments God gave to Moses and the freed people of Israel. The extra poem is a symbol of God's greatest commandment for us all—love your neighbor as you love yourself. It also represents the eleventh chapter of Hebrews, which is devoted to the theme of faith and highlights various figures who overcame the circumstances they were in because of their faith in God.

The thirteen selections in *Poems of Faith* represent the twelve apostles of Jesus and Mary Magdalene, who was also a disciple and one of the strongest followers of Christ. The three pieces in *Poems of Jesus* are to represent The Holy Trinity: God the Father, God the Son, and God the Holy Spirit. It also represents the three years that Jesus spent ministering on this Earth. Another three poems are presented for everyone that was affected by the COVID-19 pandemic, which in some way, shape, or form includes you and I. *My Testimonials* are as the title implies—my personal thoughts on what God has done for me in my life and the people that He has personally put there to guide me in some way, shape or form. *My Prayers* contains eight parts to represent the eight Beatitudes that Jesus gave to His disciples in His Sermon on the Mount.

The two poems in *Living Until the End* are in honor of the two most loyal women, and most loyal people in general, in Jesus' life: his mother Mary and Mary Magdalene.

I pray that as you read the words in this book that you are truly touched and inspired. Now more than ever, we need to bring ourselves closer to the love of Jesus Christ. The world continues to change and some people seem confused about the direction we are heading in. However, the one certainty that we have in this world and this universe is that our Lord will always be there for us, no matter what situation we find ourselves in. Keep walking in faith and God will continue to bless you always.

Be blessed,
Patrick

INTROIT

Filled with titles of famous hymns

Let me first say this as my opening thesis
Now more than ever, *I'd Rather Have Jesus*
More than silver and gold
On me, I want His love to unfold

Jesus, *I Need Thee Every Hour*
In the event that I should stray
Walk with me each and every day
I shall be blest if I *Trust & Obey*

He is there *Just When I Need Him Most*
My Father, the Son & The Holy Ghost
He accepts me *Just As I Am, Without one Plea*
So to you Lord, I should give *More Love to Thee*

I have to keep *Leaning on the Everlasting Arms*
Because *Under His Wings*, I am safe and warm
Safe in the Arms of Jesus, I am *Saved by Grace*
Oh, that sweet *Amazing Grace*

There is Power in the Blood
That we all should be washed in
The *Sweet Will of God*
Is what we need to be lost in

Whenever we need a *Sweet Hour of Prayer*
He will always lend us His ear
He will never ignore our sadness & pain
He will always *Revive Us Again*

So, *Take Time to be Holy* & *Only Trust Him*
Tis So Sweet to trust Him
He can make us *Whiter Than Snow*
Truly, *The Way of the Cross Leads Home*

What a beautiful gift to have
So, we must rejoice & be glad

Love Like Nature

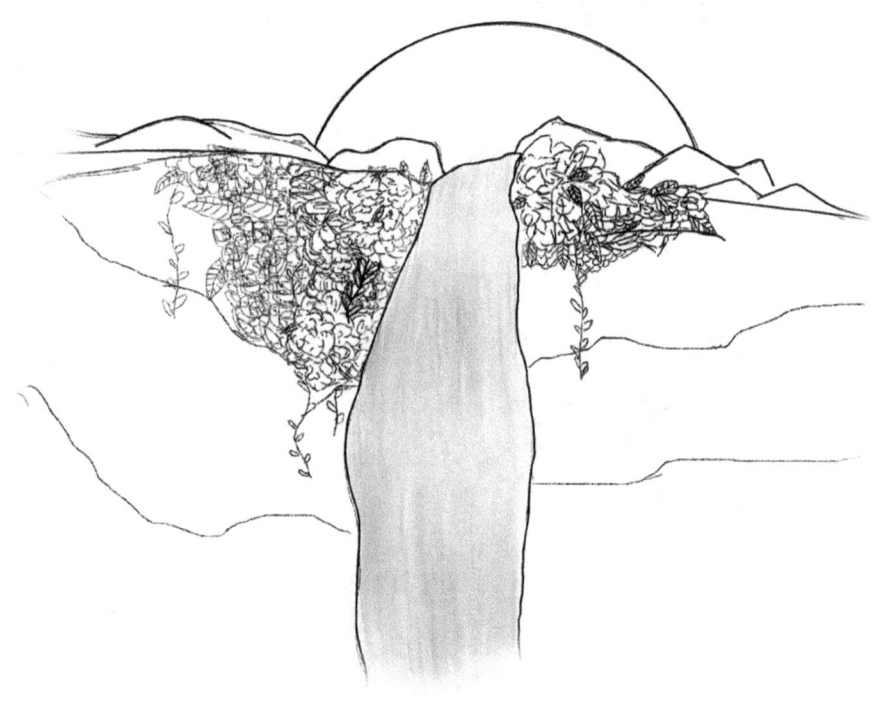

Let it Flow

Let love flow like water, flowing free
Let us drink it so it flows through you and me
Let us be like water & form one shape
Separately we are okay, but together we are great

But water is not the only thing that flows
Love is also like the wind that blows
Sometimes love flows like a cool breeze
Helping us fall in romance with ease

Sometimes love is a strong gust of wind
Telling us that more love must begin
In our homes & the streets
Let love sweep us off our feet

Allow it to throw us in a river of love
Let us go underwater & love fill our lungs
If we drown, let us drown in love
The greatest gift from God above

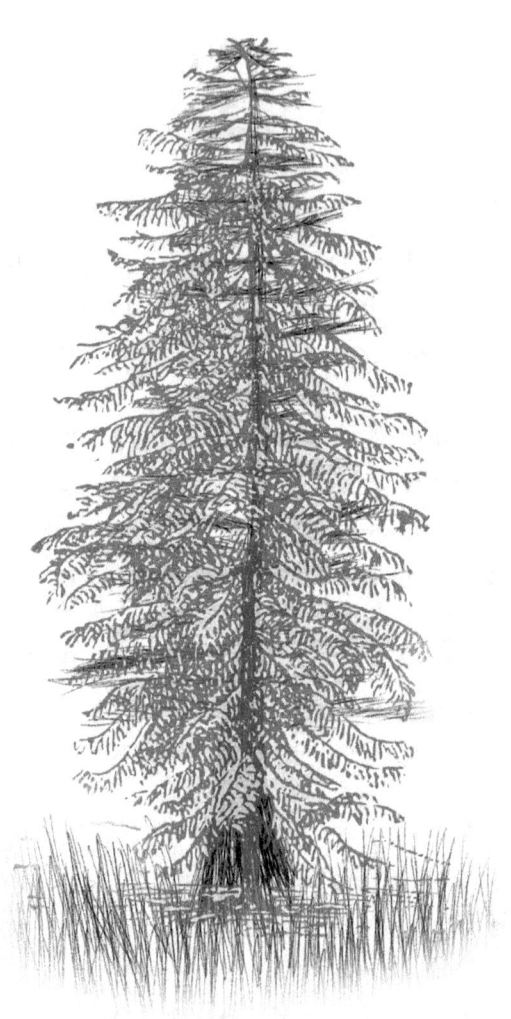

EVERGREEN

The strongest love is one that is evergreen
Like the biggest, strongest tree
The kind that grows to its highest height
That stands firm with all its might

The strongest love is one that can stand for years
Through countless storms & countless tears
Still firm like that evergreen tree
Keep it firmer than anything dreamed

Make it a wonder that others want to discover
How could a love like this come asunder?
It is because of the one thing that keeps us safe
It is simply because we have faith

Let it Roam

Love has roamed like animals since the beginning of time
Since Adam & Eve walked in the same line
As it was back then, it should once again be in the present
Let us allow love to roam like lions & elephants

Though animals nurture out of instinct,
they still know to express it
Meanwhile, day by day, human love lessens

Why can't we love like those in the jungles?
Expressing love to our spouses with a gentle nuzzle
Why can't we love like the birds in the trees?
Like mothers in their nests at rest with their seeds

Why can't we love like the fish in the water?
Swimming in cool waters as tensions grow calmer
In a way, we're not that different from
those who walk on fours
They can show us how we need to love more

So, let's nestle closer together
To make ourselves love better
From the streets to our homes
Let's allow love to gently roam

Let it Soar

For love to grow to its highest height
Let it fully grow so it can take flight
Let it soar with the greatest of ease
Let it soar through the breeze

Love should fly like an eagle
Wings spread wide
Soaring through the skies
With all kinds of pride

Let love fly like a dove, ever so peaceful
Let love come from Heaven above for all the people
Love each other more, we can all try
But first, we must let real love fly

Let it Burn

Love starts as a spark
The strike of a match that warms the heart
Making it beat faster & longer
Making the feelings we have for
someone or something stronger

So, light a candle
Warm the fireplace
Love can handle your entire space
Given for you to start a blaze

Higher & higher, allow this fire to go
Let your love continue to show
Then, when this is reduced to ember
The remnants remain for you to remember

So continue to grow & continue to learn
Continue to let love burn

The Purest Love

The purest love is like pure, white snow
The more that falls, the more it grows
Even if it shuts us in our homes
Don't let it shut us in our doubts

Let it accumulate
Let it get deeper
Let it be visible for all of love's seekers

Though snow gets stained & over time lessens
Don't let love fall into depression
Love must continue like a never ending snowstorm
Making even the coldest hearts warm

Acts of love can thaw a frozen heart
Making sure they don't beat cold and dark
Though, snow melts to water & goes apart in the sky
We can't allow love to die

We have to make sure that we keep love pure
So when we distribute it, it will be sincerely yours

Come to Him

HE IS ABLE

He can pick you up & turn your life around
Plant your feet on the firmest ground

He's always within reach in every city & town
Ready to lead us Heaven bound

He is able to help the helpless
Relieve you from all of your stresses

Although life gets tough, Jesus can do so much
Because He has the healing touch

Enough

Jesus is more valuable than any riches
More than silver and gold
He moves in mysterious ways
He does things never seen or told

He always stays by your side
Even when you've messed up
If Jesus is the only friend you have
Know that He is more than enough

He'll never leave you alone
Whether you're a child or full grown
If you ever need a favor
He'll never say "Maybe later"

He'll be there right away
Whether it's night or day
Holding your hand & leading you
All the way

BE

Jesus will *be* the peace that we need
Whenever our souls bleed
He will *be* our comfort in our pain
His truth will always *be* made plain

He will *be* our eyes when we are blind
Guide us when it's love we need to find
He will *be* there with open ears
To listen to all our fears

He will *be* the Way, Truth and Light
Making sure our future is bright
He will *be* our best friend
Until our days on Earth shall end

Then when the pearly gates we see
Waiting for us, there He will *be*

The Strongest Love

The strongest love in the world is the love of Jesus
The most real love in the world is the love of Jesus

It's stronger than a hurricane
Stronger than a tidal wave
Stronger than a tornado
Crossing over the plains

Stronger than a storm of rain, snow, sleet or hail
Jesus' love is so strong that it can never fail

It's stronger than the strongest man on Earth
No matter if he's tall, carrying much girth
Jesus' love is so strong
It has so much worth

He'll never deny you
He'll always supply you
Never take it for granted
He gives you enough to manage

Be grateful to the Lord above
For giving us the strongest love

No Divorce

Though we've cheated on Him
Been deceitful to Him
Jesus still makes sure we receive Him

He keeps taking us back in
In the midst of our sins
With Him on our side, we can only win

There's no divorce from Jesus
Though we don't deserve His love
Jesus is always faithful
The contrary defeats His purpose from above

Though His love we should take advantage
We should not take it for granted
Stay true to His word
All of His love, we can have it

Everlasting

His kind of love can never die
To match what He has, no devil can ever try

His love is stronger than cancer & stronger than AIDS
His love can heal all aches & pains

You don't need a health care plan
His love is free, so extend your hand

Though some things come in for a while, then starts passing
The love of Jesus is always everlasting

This World

This world that we're living in
Has gotten so swept in sin
They don't realize what they're doing to themselves
Caught up in increasing their wealth

People keep killing each other
Not enough people are teaching each other
Reminding us all that we should love each other

That's what Jesus said in the Bible
But instead, we worship false idols
Whether it's the Benjamins or our famous friends
All of that has to end

This world needs to come to Jesus
Once again become true believers
Because everything else will pass away
But Jesus will still stand always

What We Should Do

What we should do
Is go to Him without attitude
Admit our wrongs that we've committed for so long

Then repent for our sins so forgiveness can begin
Be humble in our words
Be humble to the Lord

Then we should proceed
To put our words in deeds
Helping those in need spread Jesus' seeds

Seeds of love
Seeds of peace
Allow faith to grow and increase

That's what we should do

How To Love

Be honest with one another
Be honest with ourselves
Be honest with Jesus

Love traditionally
Which means love unconditionally
Be faithful & be grateful to others

Be kind to everyone
Spread some charity
Always with sincerity

This is how Jesus wants us to love
Can we?

For Us

For all of us, he took our sins & faults
Nailed to a cross that stood tall
On a hill far, far away
So that we can all be saved

It should have been us, like the two thieves
Who should've been hung for our misdeeds
For all the times that we lied to our brothers
Hurt our mothers & stole from one another

Jesus would hang with His arms outstretched
Which is why He let soldiers tear His flesh
Showing that He cared about us the most
Before He finally gave up the Ghost

So to Him, we must give praise
To Him, glory we must raise
Everything He does is for us
Everyone around the world should say...

"Thank you, Jesus!!!"

God Force

So, they want to start a Space Force
A new military branch made for
Securing our place in the stars
Maybe it will help us get to Mars

Everyone in power is obsessed with expansion
I just have to ask, "What happened?"
As much as we should keep researching planets & stars
What happened to creating a force to unite our hearts?

We continue to be so focused on being better and greater
That to our fellow man, we become haters
Anyone we feel is opposition, we try to drive out
It happens at work, on the streets & even The White House

Everybody wants to be God
But, few try to seek God
Fewer try to speak God
Fewer try to preach God

So Mr. President, I make this proposition
Perhaps instead of an expensive space expedition
Turn the attention back to our country & home
Now more than ever, we need to follow a force of our own

A force that will follow Jesus Christ
Not just to sell cheap merchandise
A God Force to represent God in this current generation
We need a recurring demonstration

Of love, peace, happiness & charity
Only a God Force amidst ourselves can save us from insanity

For we wrestle not against flesh & blood
But against principalities that are treacherous
This God Force wrestles against the rulers of darkness
It wrestles against spiritual wickedness

We don't do it for publicity or politics
We do it to give each other a common lift
Our God Force doesn't need to bear arms
We already have what we need to protect us from harm

The Sword of the Spirit
The Shield of Faith
The Gospel of Peace
One day, the world will know that their ignorance must cease

Jesus died & rose again
So prosperity He can give you
Live long & prosper
May the God Force be with you

Poems of Faith and Reassurance

What You Need to Hear

Don't let Satan break you down
Let this message spread to every city, nation and town
This is something that you need to hear
To help you ease your fears & dry your tears

The God of the Earth still makes a way
With Him on your side, your spirit can't break
So the shackles on your feet, you should take them off
The blindfold on your eyes, you need to rip it off

Follow the Lord, your rock & salvation
Spread His word from nation to nation
We need to do it now without hesitation
There's no more time for procrastination

Life's too short, it's not that long
This is the reason why I wrote this song
This is what you need to hear; the message is strong
We all need to put the armor of God on

You may be knocked down & beat up
But Jesus will always pick you back up
So you could press on & never give up
You have a full life that you need to live up

So don't slip up & fall
You could have it all
If you can't run, walk
If you can't walk, crawl

But you got to keep moving
All we need is love, we need no shooting
That's all God needs to be pleased
The Devil's in fear, crumbling to his knees

So be at ease with these words that you're hearing
God's on your side; there's no need for fearing
If you feel like folding
Just turn all your cares to the King of Kings

He'll give you everything that you need
Everything's not what it seems
So don't believe the hype
There's still purpose in your life

God has so much in store
All you need to do is have faith & break forth
Conquer new horizons & do things
people may think are surprising
You're near the mountaintop; you need to keep climbing

So don't be deceived
By the lies & temptations that Satan conceives
Trust in the Lord and just believe
I just told you what you needed to hear

God Still Loves You

For everybody that has backslid on life's road
For everyone who has struggled carrying life's heavy load
No matter what sin you've committed
No matter what you're going through
God still and always loves you

You could fall down so many times
God will be there to pick you up again
Despite how many times you curse His name
He'll still bring you through the rain
His love is real & His love can heal

In spite of all wrong you do
God still loves you

DELIVERANCE

For those that have internal struggles

By grief and despair, I've been overrun
Now is the time for deliverance to come
Being born in poverty was a horrible curse
The fact that I'm black just makes things worse

I'm not ashamed of my face or race
But poverty has left a bitter taste
Not able to buy the things that my friends have
It makes me angry, jealous and sad

I yearn for deliverance
I yearn for the good life
I'm tired of the struggle
I'm looking for a better life

I yearn for deliverance
A financial deliverance
A spiritual deliverance
A personal deliverance

Deliver me Lord I pray

BETTER

I'm not what I was once was
I'm better than before
Since God came & opened the door
Allowing me to start over

Make my life anew
Now I stand before you
Better

Sometimes I stumbled
But God wouldn't let me crumble
For me, He has sometimes better planned
So He took me by the hand

Picked me up, dusted me off
Saving a soul that once was lost
Making me so much better

Sometimes it's hard for some to see
I'm not what I used to be
I'm better than I was before
The old me has gone out the door

You'll never see that person again
I'm so much better

Young People

Young people, the world is yours
God made it this way for you
There isn't anything you can't do
Anything you dream to be you could be
God will give you the grace to see

That you obtain success
Because you are truly blessed

Young people, things will get hard sometimes
Hurdles to jump over
Mountains to climb
But when times get hard
Put your trust in God

He will always be there
On Him, cast your cares

Young people, you could accomplish anything
The sky is the limit
Blessings God brings
You were born to succeed

Young people, the road won't be easy
Your heart will be broken sometimes
You'll be lied to
You'll have obstacles to overcome
But keep your faith in God

You will fulfill your dreams
Young people, just believe

In the Place of your Pain

Your life is full of pitfalls
You're at the point where you want to quit
Spending your time looking for comfort
But finding more conflict

But stand still and look up
For God shall come to you in the place of your pain

A shift is coming in your life
The sun is going to shine
The clouds will be rolled back
Happiness will come in the place of your pain

Everything you wished for will come true
Destiny will come in the place of your pain

You are at your weakest point now
Strength will come in the place of your pain

You are lost in temptation and sin
Deliverance will come in the place of your pain

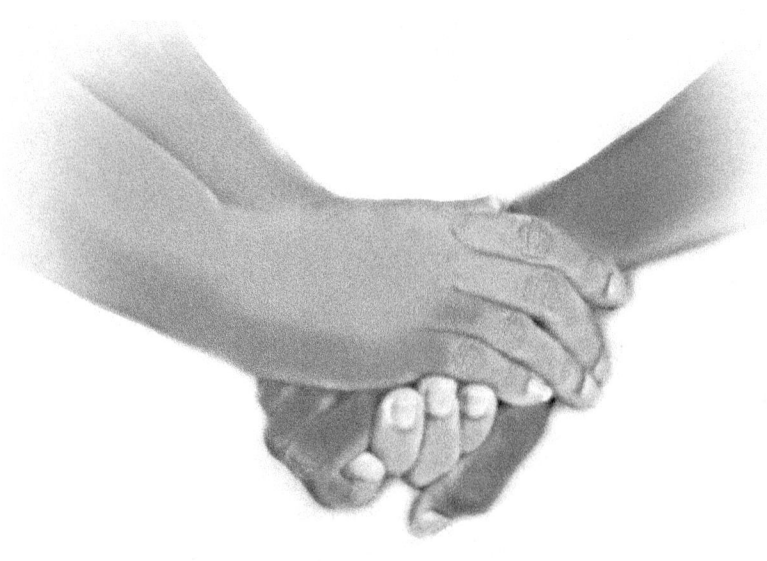

Encourage Me

A personal prayer that you can say for yourself

Encourage me to keep on walking
Encourage me to continue talking
Help me to pick myself back on my feet
Help me spread God's Word to all I meet

My soul is in danger
Filled with anger
I look in the mirror & I see a stranger

I don't know myself anymore
Everyone pulls me every which way more & more

I've lost some direction
I need your protection
Get me back on track
I need you to watch my back

I keep questioning my faith
Lord Jesus give me strength
To keep going forward & toward salvation
Do it with no hesitation

With you by my side, I cannot lose
So it's you on my side that I choose
To bring me out from whatever I'm in
Bring me out from all of my sin

Strengthen my heart
Strengthen my mind
Encourage me time after time

Remove all the sin in me
Renew a right spirit in me
Encourage me time after time

BE GRATEFUL

Be grateful to the Lord today
Be grateful that He took your sins away
Because the Lord didn't have to do what He did for you
But He did it just because He loves you

Be grateful that you were able to open your eyes
Be grateful that you could see the sky
Because some others are not like you
A blind man may cry; you know it's true

So what you need to do is be grateful

Be grateful that you have a roof over your head
Be grateful that you're sleeping in a bed
Because it didn't have to be

You could've been on the streets
Struggling to keep yourself warm
While staying away from harm
So don't be alarmed, be grateful

Be grateful that you're still alive
God has brought you through another night
Because some were not as fortunate as us
So when life gets rough, we should try not to fuss

Never be doubtful
Just be grateful

Trouble Don't Last

Trouble don't last always
Things can't stay the same
Trouble will never last
Just call on Jesus' name

One day you might sleep in tears
Drowning deep in your fears
But God always hears your cries
He will see you by and by

You don't need to worry what the next day will bring
God will always change things
Nothing can always stay the same
You just have to call on Jesus' name

Hold on to your faith & lean on His grace
God said He would see you through
He protected Daniel in the lion's den
He'll do the same for you

Walk On

No matter what struggles you face
Physical, mental, emotional, spiritual
Walk on

If you have to walk slowly, you have to keep going
Even though you may limp, still go forward
God is right next to you
He's in front of you and He's behind you

Whenever it seems like you're about to fall
God is there to help you stand
So never give up
Never stop

Stand strong brother
Stand strong sister

For Every Faith

Never be afraid to worship
Every faith has a purpose
Though they may call God a different name
Everyone loves God the same

No one should shame them
No one should defame them
You may disagree with them
But at least, keep the peace with them

Let them praise their maker
The one who shows them favor
Do not be a judge
Do not hold a grudge

For every faith has a right to live like you
Every faith has a right to give like you
For every faith deserves respect
Every faith deserves to be blessed

If not by man, definitely by God
For God's love for His children is not a façade
So, as you would ask the same for thee
Let every faith have the faith to be

FOR EVERY RACE

For every race, you are not a curse
God blessed all of you with equal worth
He wants all races to share the earth
Lift each other up when one is hurt

Every race is beautiful
Every race is blessed
Every race is phenomenal
We shouldn't compare which is best

We are all lovely in God's eyes
We should all walk by God's side
The Bible says we shouldn't judge
So, let's not use race to hold a grudge

God loves us all the same
So, let us do the same
Let's not subject each other to shame
Too many times we've played that game

As one race, the truth we must seek
For God doesn't see nationality or creed
God doesn't see red & yellow or black & white
We are all beautiful in His light

So, let's just be His children
If we have faith as one race, we'll always win

There Will Be Days . . .

*Dedicated to anybody who has lost
someone that they truly loved*

There will be days when you cry
Sad that you never got to say goodbye
There will be days when you want one more chance
To see your loved one if just for a glance

There will be days when you feel pain
Anger & confusion plaguing your brain
This may happen as the days go by
Leaving you with nothing to do but cry

However, there will be days when you reminisce
On every kind word, hug and kiss
It will fill your heart with bliss
Making you realize there was nothing better than this

There will be days that though you are sad
You will say "God, thank you for what I had"
The gift you gave me was genuine & true
This special person loved me, just like you

There will be days in the coming years
That through mixed emotions, it becomes more clear
That your special someone ran a good race
Now, they have gone to a better place

They are resting comfortably in God's grace
Be sure, they will save you a space
Their life was not lived in vain
Hold your faith, for you will see them again

Poems of Jesus

Who Am I? (I am God!)

I'm the Creator of all mankind
In me, peace you'll find
I am your Savior & your King
I'm worth more than all the bling bling

Your souls I will redeem
My word is true and not a dream
You just have to believe in me
'Cause I am your Everything

I am the First & the Last
I am your present, future & your past
I am the Rock in a weary land
I am the strength that helps you stand

I'm Alpha & Omega, Beginning & End
I am your best friend
I'm present everywhere at all times
So from me, you cannot hide

I'm a Fortress when you're stressed
Helping you pass every test
I'm a Counselor when you're in need
Bring all your cares to me

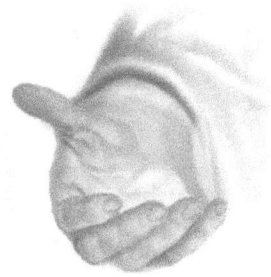

Because I'm your Shepherd & you're my sheep
I'll never leave you behind so don't you weep

I am the Light & Salvation
I am seen from nation to nation
I am all powerful & all wise
I know all your thoughts, so don't be surprised

I am the Lord of Hosts
Who rests with my Son & the Holy Ghost
I am the I Am
No one can do what I can

There is no one like me
If there is, they'll never be seen
Because no other exists
So I want you to know this

Now if you don't know me by now
Let me tell you who I am
I am God

Superstar

Jesus Christ is the world's first true superstar
But He never drove around in a fancy car
He just wanted to do God's will
So your soul could remain still

He was the first to be followed wherever he walked
People hung on His words whenever He talked
They wanted to come & see
The man from Galilee

The way He performs His miracles
Everyone saw them as unbelievable
Incredible
Inconceivable

He healed the sick without a medical degree
Making the lame man walk & the blind man see
He may not star in movies or on TV
But He is all that we really need

He doesn't party all night
He tries to lead us all into the light
He always made headline news
Whether or not to believe in Him, we have to choose

He doesn't need a TV show to let us know
That walking with Him is the way to go
He doesn't need a silver screen to get our attention
Oh yes, I forgot to mention

He doesn't need to wear designer clothes
Because He is whiter than snow
He always shimmers and glows
So we need to know

Jesus Christ is the Way, the Truth and the Light
Bringing us through the darkness of night
Into the brightest of days
So always give Him praise

The Powers of Jesus

Who else can tell Satan to get behind him?
I won't fall into your sin
Who else can get thousands to listen to His words?
More than a school teacher trying to get kids to learn

Before any politician
He was able to get all to stop & listen
So you need to believe this
Nobody has the powers of Jesus

Who has the power to heal diseases?
Even turning cynics into believers
Who can stand in the middle of the ocean & calm the storm?
Who else can drive demons from our homes?

Who can make twelve men help carry His Word?
That's more powerful than carrying a sword
Who can speak in parables to get His message across?
That if you believe in God, you can't have a loss

Who could turn water into wine?
And make it taste so fine
But what tastes much sweeter is that He's mine

Who else could raise the dead?
Feed 5,000 with 2 fish & 5 loaves of bread
Who else could walk on water?
Any imitations shouldn't even bother

Who else could suffer & die for our sins?
In order to save us from within
So we could lift up our heads
Because only He could rise from the dead

Not Superman, not Batman
Nobody can do what He can
Not Spider Man or Iron Man
They don't have the whole world in their hands

He's stronger than the mighty Thor
He's the one you should really call for
Shining brighter than a Green Lantern in darkest night
Evil must bow down in His sight

He'll race to your aid faster than The Flash
Protect you like Wonder Woman's bracelets from a blast
Have faith in Him as strong as Steve Rogers
If you need Jesus, just holler

He'll come to us all
To nurture and feed us
The greatest hero of all time
Is named Jesus

Dedicated to the Victims of COVID-19

Every one of us was affected in one way or another by the Coronavirus pandemic of 2020. Some of you that are reading this may have lost someone to COVID-19 or know someone that lost a member of their family to it. You may have been diagnosed with the disease yourself and overcame it. You may have been a first responder on the front lines treating those that were affected by this terrible disease or a teacher who had to teach remotely when schools were shut down. Children were sad that they could not see their friends in school or in the playground. We all felt bad because we could not go out and socialize with our friends. All of the things that we sometimes take for granted, we were not able to do.

All in all, it has been and still is a trying time for all of us.

Through it all, there was hopefully one thing that came through amidst all of this – we need to get closer together and not push each other apart. We need to appreciate those around us and give them love and comfort. More importantly, we need to get closer to God and increase our faith. Hopefully, these poems provide some comfort to you.

From a Distance

From a distance, I wonder
Is this the other way we will discover
That we really need to be closer together
Cords of love should be tightened & not severed

Now from a distance, we yearn to get close
We want the spaces between us to be closed
But when our distances get closer, let's
not push each other away
Let us keep our hearts in God come what may

In good days & bad days
In happy and sad days
Let us continue to be better
Let God in love bind us together

When This Passes

When this passes, let us not be the same
Let us show more respect to each other's names

When this passes, let us slowly heal
Let us, to each other, be more & more real

When this passes, let us not go back
Let's say to each other that we have each other's back

When this passes, the one thing I want to come true
Is for everyone to say 'I love you'

Appreciated

For the first responders, teacher, supermarket workers, volunteers, teachers, daycare workers, and everybody that assisted others in some way, shape or form during the COVID-19 Pandemic

Derived from a poem I wrote in my first book,
PoEmotions: Poems of life, love, faith and all emotions

For always putting in some overtime
If you sometimes feel like it's just an oversight
Always keep a positive mind

For spending your time working your fingers to the bone
Only to do the same when you get home
I just want you to know

You're appreciated each & every day
In every single way
You're appreciated always

For putting your bodies on the line
Having to stay on an endless grind
To put food on the table for your kids
Keeping up the house where your family lives

For always answering the call of duty
When others in the other direction would be moving
You are soldiers in your own uniforms
Always stay true to form

If you never knew it before, you know now
Of your selfless service, we as a people are proud
No wonder some kids want to grow up to be like you
Because your actions and service is true

Just know that you are always appreciated

My Testimonials

Church on the Corner

My church on the corner is my second home
Where my voice to sing was grown
This little church raised me when I was a baby
After five years away from it, a force was gravitating

Bringing me back to this place on Sundays
So that God can guide me into Monday

I started as a Joy Bell & then I would grow
Singing *Fill My Cup & Let it Overflow*
I learned to play the piano & I never looked back
In church, I started speaking about my pride of being Black

Eventually, I moved to the organ
Tunes to God for God go soaring
Straight to Heaven & His listening ears
Playing loud so God is listening clear

My church on the corner is my refuge
Protecting me from becoming a recluse
There, I can go and pray
In the hopes that my fears & tears will wash away

There, I can give my all to You
There, I can let my troubles fall on You
I know you're in more places than my corner church
You are always there to comfort me when I'm sore or hurt

So, I must give you praise
Dear Lord, I will love You always

Give Me Strength

Lord, I often get sad
I often get depressed
I often feel alone
I often feel like giving in to all those negative feelings

I know that my future will be better
But, my present is so hard
My present is so complicated
My present is so overwhelming at times

I feel weak
Lord, give me strength
If I start to break
Give me faith

When I cry, help me wipe my tears
When I fret, help me shed my fears
When I feel that there is no way
Remind me that You are The Way

Guide my days, no matter the length
But always, give me strength

High on God

Following the Lord, I want to be convicted
Because His blessings have made me so gifted
I must admit to you first that I'm addicted
For the Word of God will get your spirit lifted

So I got to have it
I got to grab it
I can't doubt it
I can't live without it

So when your soul gets drifted
Think of the place where heavenly bliss is
Where you don't have to think about sin
And get happiness within

He's better than any medicine that a doctor can prescribe
When you experience how good God is, it'll blow your mind
He's more powerful than any injection
Giving you protection & leading you in the right direction

You don't have to take trips on LSD or ecstasy
Just go to G.O.D.
Stop puffing on that weed and just look & see
Jesus will give you everything that you need

You don't need cocaine to try to ease your pain
More wicked things will just build up in your brain
Jesus is simple and is plain
He can give you pleasures immeasurable again & again

The only high that I ever want to get is from You
The only kind of supplier I should want is Your truth
Because you brought me out of so many situations
I don't need to take street dope & start having hallucinations

Whenever I need a fix
I should turn to You God
The only thing I ever want to get high of
Is You - God

Dear Godfather

In honor of my godfather, Elder Irvin Lyrell George

Dear Godfather

It's been nearly two years since you went away
It's been nearly two years since God
called you by His side to stay
Your race is fully run
He has said to you, "Well done"

You were humble & always praised God's name
Hopefully one day I can be the same

Always willing to learn
Always willing to serve
Always having my spirit burn
With a love for the Lord, a love worth living for

You praised the Lord even in your worst days
Now, you are sailing by His side as His first mate
Gathering those who share your similar fate
To dwell forever behind those heavenly gates

So for now, I say, "So long"
The world is so different now that you are gone
However, I will never let you part
You are always with me in my heart

My Prayers

911 Emergency II

Derived from a poem I wrote in my 1st book, *PoEmotions:
Poems of life, love, faith and all emotions*

911 Emergency
Jesus set our spirits free
Then help the world to see
That your love is all they need

To move from day to day
All they have to do is pray
Humbly with no delay
Then you'll show them the way

To love, peace & happiness
Freedom from everyday stress
Using all their intellect
To do their best to progress

To make this world a better place
For every gender, every race
Then their sins you will erase
'Cause you've redeemed us by your grace

But some folks don't want to know you
So they take you out of schools
Now I say that's not cool

They're hiding God's truth from the youth
And because they don't know the truth
They look for a gun to learn to shoot

Children are the most precious in God's eyes
Tell them to keep their eyes on the prize
Then they'll know that you care
Happiness they will share

So once again, here's my prayer

911 Emergency
Jesus save the community
Bring us all to unity
So we can be what you called us to be

Come to Me

Come to me Lord Jesus
Come to me Lord Jesus
I am tired and in pain
Show me some happiness again

Come to me with no delay
I don't need you tomorrow
I need you today

My life is a struggle
I see nothing but trouble
Lord I need a resolution
You are the only solution

My heart is in pain
I need shelter from the rain
I don't need you later
I need you now

My road is getting rougher
Each day is getting tougher
Don't know how much more I can take
Carrying a load on my shoulders, heavy as boulders

It feels like I'm gonna break
But Lord I know you'll deliver me
From whatever it is I'm in
So Lord deliver me right away

Come to me Lord Jesus
Come to me Lord Jesus
I am tired and in pain
Show me some happiness again

Come to me with no delay
I don't need you tomorrow
I need you today

For My Family

Dear Lord, bless my mother
Thank you for having her be the one to raise me

Though at times we have differences
There are always instances
That she gives a kind word of advice
Acting through a kind Lord that's nice

Bless my father, though we're far apart
Thank you for making space for him in my heart
Bonds have been able to form
Because of you Lord
Both of us are forever grateful

Bless my grandmother
Bring relief to her pain
That one day, she'll find her smile again
If the day comes that You call her to rest
I take comfort that in You, she's blessed

These I ask in Your name
Amen

For My Friends

Bless all of my friends; they know who they are
Bless them whether they are near or far

Keep them in safe travels wherever they go
Your grace to others, let them show

Always shine Your grace on them
So others can see You through them

On the streets or on the job
Remind them that they're children of God

When the time comes, bless them with love
Because their blessings will be showered from above

Amen

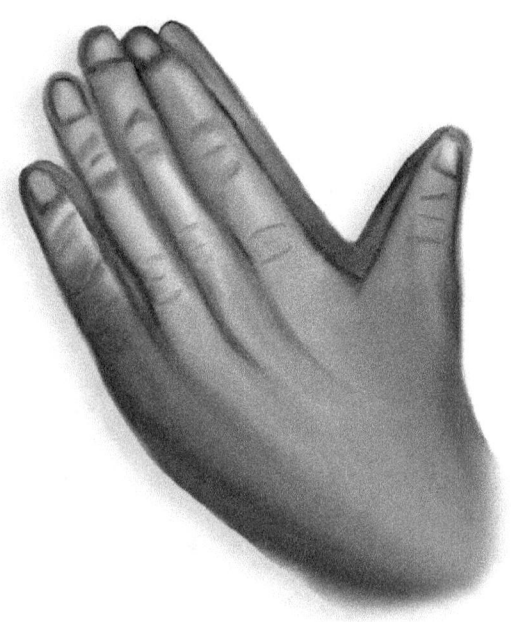

FOR THE DEAD

Dear Lord, bless those souls that have gone to rest
Bless those who stood the test
Those who aged gracefully or died premature
All of them are now safely Yours

They're away from a world of pain and sorrow
In a place where the Sun always shines tomorrow
To those families who may still be in grief
Bring about sweet relief

That one day they will once again meet
Together to walk the golden streets

Amen

For Kendall

Dear Lord, bless my goddaughter
Bless her as she continues to grow
Bless her mind with what she comes to know

Let her keep walking in Your light
In time, she'll learn to walk by faith
Not by sight

Allow her to be blessed by good company
Let her presence & essence to others be comforting

When she gives a radiant smile
Let it show others that she's Your child

Thank you for placing her in my life
She makes my little light shine bright

Keep her safe from all harms
Let the world be warmed by her charms

This I ask in Your name

Amen

For America

Jesus, bless America
We're a nation lost
Into death's hands, more lives are tossed

Everyone is running around
Pointing fingers
Allowing hate to still linger

We're caught in crimes from rape to extortion
Babies don't see life 'cause mama had an abortion
America has taken You out of schools
Most want nothing to do with Your Good News

Please enlighten Your nation with truth
Allowing it all to shine through
You're the only one that can really make America great again
Allow us to make amends

This prayer I raise to you

Amen

For the World

Grab this world into Your hands
Allow every man to understand
That love is what it needs
They need to plant more seeds

Love can conquer hate
For Your love is great
Your love conquers all
At Your feet, evil must fall

So to You, I pray for this entire world
Every man & woman, every boy & girl
Regardless of race or religion
We are all one human race with no divisions

I pray for all of this world's conflicts to cease
Let this world come together in peace

War & murder is not the answer
You are

Diplomats are not the answer
You are

Amen

For My Unborn Children

Lord, bless my children not yet conceived
Bless my kids that I have yet to receive
But I know that the day will come
When I'll have a daughter or a son

Let them be a sunbeam for You
Let them always gleam for You
Let the sparkle in their eyes
Or a smile on their face
Remind me of Your grace

When my children do grow
Let them come to know
That they are really Yours
It's You that they are really living for

This I ask in Your name

Amen

Living Until the End

I've Got More Living to Do

When your life seems hard
And you scream to God
About all your troubles
While you try to hustle in the everyday struggle

People try to push you over the edge
So much stress filled in your head
You try to find an escape, but you think it may be too late
So your mind begins to be filled with thoughts of hate

I can relate

You want to throw it all away
But I'm telling you that tomorrow brings a brighter day
All that you need to do is go to God and say
"I put my trust in you. I know that you will make a way"

So the message that I bring to you
Hold on, you've got much more living to do

I've suffered all the pain
Walked through storm and rain
Anger filled my veins as I began to complain
That God's love for me just wasn't the same

But then God spoke to me
He said, "Put your faith in me"
Just believe in me & I won't deceive thee
I'll help you push so you can fulfill your destiny

From that day on, I've tried to follow in His light
When I strayed to the wrong, He set me back to the right
Now I could move forward with my life
So one day I have a house with kids and a wife

Now he'll do the same for you
He'll take your troubled life and make it brand new

So, it's time to choose

Which way do you want to go?
If Satan creeps in your life, shake him off & say "No!"
But that choice I'm going to leave to you
'Cause now I've got much more living to do

Surviving the World

I am young, but I have lived through so much
I have seen that the world can have a callous touch
People suffering injustice without a care
Getting hateful expressions with just a stare

We should be moving forward
Instead, we are moving back
Everyone keeps searching for a reason
Emotions & opinions change like seasons

But, even seasons change with stability
Our way of life experiences more fragility
Cracks continue to form
Stress makes us tired and worn

Never would have thought that when I was born
That 31 years later, I would see so much scorn
Although at times I have felt worn
I remind myself that I have made it through storms

Throughout my personal history
I have achieved personal victories
Though I have yet to complete my race
I have made this far by faith

My last victory will be the sweetest
After all my strength is depleted
My Jesus, I hope to meet Him
My Jesus, I hope to greet Him

What a wonderful day that will be
When Jesus comes calling for me
From the world, I shall be free
Forevermore, I shall be free

About the Author

Patrick Laurence Charles Meade is a teacher, musician, poet, songwriter and script writer. He has a Bachelor's Degree in Childhood Education from The City College of New York. Patrick is the assistant musician at St. Paul's Progressive Methodist Church in the Bronx, New York. It's a position he has proudly served in for over fifteen years.

Patrick enjoys listening to gospel music, rap (mostly old school rap from the late 80s to the mid 2000s, but still has love for some of today's artists) and R&B. He also enjoys writing his own original songs, poems, scripts and short skits. Some of Patrick's skits have been performed at St. Paul's Church and were well received. He has also performed some of his original songs in church, which were also well received. Most recently, he's been working on manuscripts for future projects.

Preceding this book are *PoEmotions: Poems of life, love, faith and all emotions* (2017), *PoEmotions Black History: Our Origins, Our Struggles, Our Future* (2018) and *Flowers Grow & Butterflies Fly and other short poems for children*, (2019).

Patrick was born & raised in the Bronx, New York, where he still lives.

Titles scheduled to release in 2021: *PoEmotions Black History for Kids* and *PoEmotions Black History: The Deeper The Roots*

Faith is the victory that overcomes the world
To God be the glory, great things He has done!

Now more than ever, the world needs to lean more on our faith. With all that surrounds us, we have to bring each other together in love and harmony. The key to doing that is by having faith.

We need to increase our faith in God, without whom we can do nothing and we would be nothing. Through faith, there is nothing that we cannot do or accomplish. My hope in putting this special collection together is to try conveying this to you, the reader. Regardless of your denomination of worship, these poems are still worth reading and could hopefully help you get through whatever circumstance you may be going through. So, like a hymn says, *be very sure that your anchor holds and grips the solid rock.*

www.ingramcontent.com/pod-product-compliance
Lightning Source LLC
Chambersburg PA
CBHW052109110526
44592CB00013B/1534